MW01639970

To Mike & Jo.

Family is an important part of life. I am blessed to be a part of yours.

Love

Arlene.

Buon Appetito

Momma's Christmas Cookbook

Classic Italian Family Recipes to Inspire New Holiday Traditions

ARLENE FRANCO-IAQUINTO

Library of Congress Cataloging-in-Publication Data

Momma's Christmas Cookbook: Classic Italian Family Recipes to Inspire New Holiday Traditions

Arlene Franco-Iaquinto

Cover and interior photos from iStockphoto, Shutterstock and the author's personal collection.

p. cm.
ISBN: 978-0-9904211-0-8
Library of Congress Control Number: 2014942957

H14
10 9 8 7 6 5 4 3 2 1
First Edition
Printed and Bound in the United States of America

A publication of TriMark Press, Inc.
368 South Military Trail
Deerfield Beach, FL 33442
800.889.0693
www.TriMarkPress.com

www.MommasChristmas.com

Dedication

For my Mom and Dad, Carl and Frances, who taught me to love

To my late husband, Al, who gave me so much love

To my husband, Tony, who completes my love

Arlene Franco-Iaquinto

Author's Note

The purpose of this cookbook is to reflect on days gone by, to carry on a tradition and to share these recipes with other families. I have no special knowledge of food but write this from a very personal perspective. It is not meant for chefs or food professionals. It is written for the person who remembers what her mother or grandmother put on the table as the family's traditional Christmas dishes.

To many Italians, Christmas Eve (*La Virgilia de Natale*), is a night of feasting with family and friends. Until today, it remains a time for carrying on family traditions. It is traditions that keep us together. Christmas becomes more than a holiday or a holy day — it is the time of the year when families get together to renew family ties, share past memories and create new ones.

The ritual of the Christmas Eve meal evolved from the Catholic tradition of abstaining from meat at certain times of the year. Today, the church requires abstinence only on Ash Wednesday and Fridays during Lent. However, many older Catholics may recall when Fridays were meatless days. This was a day to show penance and unity with Christ's suffering on the cross. Italian Christmas Eve is a symbol of respect.

There are many different customs as to the number of fishes that are served. The number three symbolizes the Holy Trinity, four represents the Gospels, seven stands for the sacraments of the Catholic faith and twelve represents Christ's twelve apostles. Whatever is served, it's the tradition that sparks the magic of bringing together friends and families celebrating a night of good food, smiles, hugs and kisses, a great combination that would please even Christ himself.

Mommas' Christmas Tradition

I also dedicate this book to the memory of my mother-in-law, Lucia Franco, who passed away in 1974. She filled our Christmases with joy and love of the holiday season. I remember those Christmases as special times filled with laughter and the excitement of our family celebrating time together.

Lucia's Christmas dinner was not a simple meal. Preparations began days in advance. Food was purchased from specialty stores on Arthur Avenue in the Little Italy section of the Bronx.

Lucia was a natural cook who never needed recipes. She would add a dash of salt, half a handful of sugar, or two "fingers" of milk. Her eyes, keen sense of smell and taste buds knew what the recipe called for. Her baking filled the house with the aromas of holiday cookies: struffolis, anginetts, and of course her famous cinnamon and walnut cookies. She hid the freshly-baked cookies in shoeboxes lined with waxed paper. We always felt challenged to find them and eat as many as possible ahead of time.

After elaborate preparations, she would gather her family (consisting of two daughters, two sons, their spouses and her precious grandchildren) for Christmas Eve and Christmas day meals. I can still picture the family around the huge old-fashioned wooden table with claw feet, set with her precious handmade lace tablecloth from her native Naples, Italy.

It is my purpose to share with you those dishes that she served with such care and love so that your holidays will also be special.

About Momma

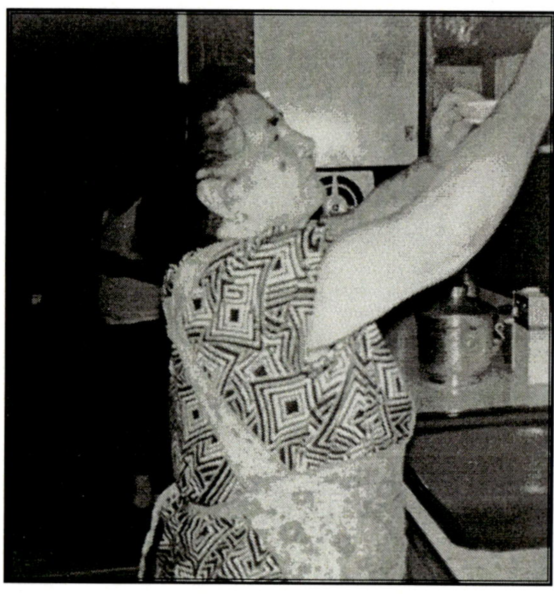

Lucia was born in the year 1911 in a small farming region of Italy. She grew up on a farm in the town of Sarno. I believe that is why Lucia was such a great cook; she understood the relationship of the earth and nature in all its natural wonders. She related that experience through her cooking.

After a short courtship, Lucia married Alfonso in 1929 and they came to America on their honeymoon. She had the longest honeymoon I know because she did not return to her native Italy until 1956 for a short visit. Lucia never learned to read or write, but her keen sense and brave spirit equaled that of any formal education. It amazed me to think how brave she must have been to leave her family and friends and come to America. She was unable to speak the language and yet thrived in this new land. She adopted this country and became a United States citizen, and she was extremely proud of it. Her human spirit is one that should be admired.

Momma's
Christmas Menu

Momma's

Christmas Eve Dinner

Momma's
Christmas Day Meal

Momma's

Holiday Cookies and Cakes

(Continued)

Momma's
FAMILY FAVORITES

Momma's

Hot Appetizers

Delicious Soups

Momma's
MEAT & FISH DISHES

Momma's

Favorite Pastas

Momma's

Classic Desserts

Favorite Drinks

Momma's
Christmas Eve Dinner

Baked Clams

1 lb. fresh minced clams
1 dozen clam shells
1 c. seasoned bread crumbs
2 cloves of chopped garlic
1 tsp. lemon juice
½ c. extra virgin olive oil
⅛ c. chopped fresh Italian parsley
¼ c. grated Locatelli-brand parmigiano
paprika

Mix clams, seasoned bread crumbs, garlic, parsley, grated cheese. Add clam juice, lemon juice and olive oil for moisture. Scoop mixture in clam shells, sprinkle with paprika and bake at 300° for approximately 25 minutes.

Mussels Fra Diavolo

1 lb. mussels in shells (scrubbed, beards removed)
1 tbsp. olive oil
⅛ tsp. crushed red pepper flakes
⅛ tsp. oregano
2 tsp. parsley, finely chopped
2-3 garlic cloves
¼ c. bottled clam juice
¼ c. white wine
2 c. fresh or canned tomatoes

Sauté garlic and pepper flakes in olive oil. Add tomatoes, parsley, oregano and simmer for 10 minutes. Add clam juice, wine and mussels on low heat for 5 minutes or until mussels open.

Baccala Salad

1 lb. dried baccala
1 jar or can black olives
1 jar or can green olives
1 jar or can red roasted peppers
1 jar pepperoncini peppers
1 jar cherry peppers
½ c. chopped celery
4 cloves of garlic
½ c. extra virgin oil
¼ c. wine vinegar

Dried baccala must be soaked in cold water 2 days before cooking. Change water at least 2 times a day and store in refrigerator. More frequent water changes will allow more salt to be removed from the fish. Boil baccala and cool in refrigerator. Chop pepper, olives and celery.

Flake the fish and add to ingredients. Add garlic, oil and vinegar. Serve cold.

Calzone

(Onion Pie)

3 lbs. onion, sliced
1 can anchovies
1 can green olives, pitted and sliced
2 1 lb. pieces of prepared pizza dough

Fry onions. When they are almost cooked, add anchovies and stir until anchovies melt. Add olives and cook for a few minutes. Grease pan, lay out one piece of pizza dough in bottom of pan overlapping it over the edges of the pan. Add onion mixture. Cover with other piece of dough, fold over the ends and pinch to make sure it doesn't open while baking. Bake at 350° for about 40 minutes until golden brown.

Spaghetti Calamari

2 lbs. calamari (*cleaned*)
1 28 oz. can of crushed
tomato puree
½ c. red wine
1 small onion, chopped
1 tbsp. chopped parsley
3 cloves of garlic
¼ c. olive oil
pinch of oregano

Cut calamari into rings. Sauté them in garlic, onion and oil for 1 minute. Add tomatoes, oregano, parsley and wine.

Simmer for 5 minutes. Calamari should be tender. Do not overcook calamari or it will get chewy. Pour over 1 pound of linguine.

Spaghetti Aglio é Olio

(Garlic and Oil)

1 lb. linguine
¼ c. extra virgin olive oil
6 cloves of garlic *more garlic the better the taste*
2 anchovy fillets, *chopped*
¼ c. fresh chopped Italian parsley
(*½ c. chopped walnuts or pine nuts optional)*
½ c. water
¼ c. chicken stock
(*chopped red pepper optional*)

Heat oil in skillet over medium heat. Sauté garlic, anchovies, parsley and chicken broth. Bring to a boil and cook for about 3 minutes. You may add some of the pasta water if you desire a juicier sauce. Add walnuts and pour over linguine. Sprinkle with black pepper.

Linguine with White Clam Sauce

1 lb. linguine
¼ c. virgin olive oil
4 cloves of chopped garlic
1 lb. chopped fresh clams
1¼ c. clam juice
¼ c. white wine
¼ c. fresh chopped parsley
fresh ground pepper
to taste
dried red pepper flakes
(*optional*)

Bring to a boil a large pot of water for the linguine. While the pasta water is heating, heat the oil and garlic in a medium saucepan, stirring occasionally, until the garlic begins to release its aroma, about 3 minutes. Add the clams, broth, and white wine, stirring lightly to mix. Simmer for 10 minutes or until clams are cooked (clam shells open). Add the linguine to the boiling water and cook until *al dente* about 8 to 10 minutes. Pour about a third of the sauce into a large pasta bowl, add the cooked drained pasta and quickly toss. You may want to add some of the pasta water for a more juicy sauce. Pour the remaining sauce over the pasta and mix. Add salt and pepper to taste. Dried red pepper flakes may be added for a more spicy flavor.

Pickled Eels

(Anguilla)

1 lb. eels, cleaned and skinned
½ c. extra virginolive oil
4 cloves of garlic
½ c. red wine vinegar
¼ c. chopped fresh parsley

Fish can be either fried in flour or boiled, depending on your preference. After cooking the fish, marinate in oil, vinegar, garlic and parsley. Marinate in refrigerator for one day before serving.

Fried Baccala, Calamari, Flounder and Shrimp

2 lbs. fish
1 c. flour
2 garlic cloves
1 large egg
parsley, lemon
salt and pepper
to taste

Variation:
¾ cup bread crumbs
1 large egg
1 tbsp. milk
salt and pepper

Dip fish in egg and milk. Roll into bread crumbs. Heat oil until hot. Fry until golden brown and fish is tender. Shrimp is ready when they turn pink. Do not overcook, fish will get chewy. One pound of fish will serve approximately 3 to 4 people.

Momma and Family

Momma's love of family was the most important part of her life. The relationship with her husband was one of mutual respect. She was a caring person and truly nurtured her four children. Her home was also a great source of pride and the kitchen was her joy. Momma was always in the kitchen preparing something. She very rarely used canned or store-bought supplies. Everything was prepared from scratch and she always used fresh vegetables.

Every summer, Momma would buy bushels of tomatoes and jar them to make her own tomato sauce. She would place tomatoes in boiling water for a few seconds, peel off the skin, and place them in the press to strain the seeds out. Fresh basil was always added to the jars.

Momma also preserved the best vinegar eggplant. Poppa naturally made his own wine. In the basement, fifty mason jars would line the long table ready to be filled and stored. Italian basements or "the downstairs" are like no other basements. It was used as a preparation and storage room for the bountiful harvest of tomatoes, basil and fresh vegetables to be jarred and used throughout the year.

Jarred food would line the shelves while herb plants hung from the ceiling drying out. Basil, Italian parsley and hot peppers adorned the ceiling. The utensils used for preparing the food were hung up. Large metal bowls and large tubs were meticulously maintained and stored, conveniently waiting to be used. Of course the wine press had a section of the basement all of its own and Poppa was the only person who used it.

Besides the wine, they made homemade liquors. Among Momma's specialty liquors were Strega, Grappa and Rock and Rye made with grain alcohol, citrus fruit and rock candy. They were better than any store-bought brand on the market today.

Shrimp Scampi

1½ lb. large cleaned shrimp
3-4 cloves of garlic
2 tsp olive oil
¼ lb. butter
1/4 c. chopped parsley
1/2 c. white wine
1 tsp. lemon juice
salt and pepper to taste
½ tsp. red pepper flakes

In a saute pan heat olive oil and butter until melted. Add garlic and red pepper flakes and sauté until garlic turns a light golden color. Add the shrimp and wine to pan and stir. Place shrimp evenly in pan and let cook for one minute. Turn shrimp over for even cooking. Cook until wine boils down. Remove from stove. Add parsley, lemon juice and black pepper. Serve alone or over pasta.

Escarola Imbottita

(Stuffed Escarole)

1 head of escarole
1 jar capers
3 cloves of chopped garlic
1 can of sliced black olives
1 can anchovies
1 tbsp. pine nuts
¼ c. extra virgin olive oil
¼ c. chopped fresh parsley

Wash escarole well. Spread escarole leafs apart from center of head keeping the middle in tact. Stuff with caper, olives, anchovies, garlic and parsley. Fold up the leafs and tie together with white string. Steam in pot with ¼ cup of water and sprinkle olive oil for taste over escarole. Simmer for 10 minutes or until escarole is tender.

Cold Broccoli with Lemon

Steam broccoli florets in pot until tender. Cool in refrigerator. Arrange on plate and sprinkle 2 cloves of chopped garlic, the juice of one lemon and sprinkle with olive oil. Serve with lemon wedges on sides of plate.

Salad

Salad can be a gallery of greens enhanced by lively, imaginative dressings. You could use most any kind of lettuce with a mixture of various herbs and spices. For better flavor, always use extra virgin olive oil, a squirt of lemon juice and a tablespoon of vinegar. Vinegar can be wine vinegar or balsamic.

Teasing Momma

Momma was a small woman, four feet nine inches tall and well rounded. Her home atttire was always proper: a house dress, stockings, shoes and full apron. The apron draped around her body outlining her belly. She had a great sense of humor, and would use it to her advantage. She was a teaser; she knew how to give and take, but it always came from love.

Her son, Butch, had the same sense of humor. They complement each other. Butch would sneak up behind her and untie her apron strings. When she sat on the kitchen chair he'd tie the loose strings to the back of the chair. When she attempted to get up, the chair would follow.

We all remember times she disciplined her sons. In broken English she'd shout, "get the "ell outa here you noja listen to me anyway!" There were always light-hearted exchanges between mother and sons. Of course, Butch had to get the last tease in by picking her up off the floor and sitting her down on the kitchen counter top. With her short, stocky body, Lucia could not get down without assistance. I still recall her sitting there, with her belly jumping up and down, reflecting her laughter calling out, "Butch....Butchy, eh coma backa, getta me down from here." With a smile on his face, Butch would walk out the door. To this day, I don't know how she got down from the kitchen counter.

Momma's
CHRISTMAS DAY MEAL

Dinner at Momma's

Momma's evening meals always consisted of a first (*primi piatti*) and a second (*secondi piatti*) dish — usually a pasta dish followed by a meat dish. Her pasta dishes were full of flavor and she was creative in preparing them. She never used anything frozen or canned. Fresh vegetables, olive oil and an abundance of garlic flavored her dishes. As far as I'm concerned, garlic is the essence of Italian cooking: the more the better.

Her pasta dishes were considered peasant dishes. They consisted of pasta with broccoli, macaroni and cauliflower, pasta with peas and pasta fagioli. Today, in the average restaurant, they are considered gourmet dishes.

Since pasta was prepared almost every night, no Italian would use just one kind of pasta and Momma was no different. There were a variety of sizes and shapes, so that you felt you were eating something different each night. There was spaghetti, linguine, rigatoni, ziti, buccatini, elbows, orzo and Momma's favorite cresta de gallo (chicken heads). Her homemade ravioli was a culinary delight. I never wrote down her recipe, but I can see her as if it were yesterday rolling out the dough then pressing down with a glass to get the perfect circle, spooning the ricotta mixture on each circle, covering the dough and then with a fork pressing all around the ravioli to seal them closed.

They were as light as a feather, the best I've ever eaten. The second dish, the meat portion was smaller. It was a way of feeding your family economically. Years ago this was the way to eat, probably out of necessity. Whatever it was, they somehow knew, smaller portions and less fat is much healthier.

Antipasto

Antipasto is the Italian equivalent of an appetizer. The word *antipasto* literally translates "before the pasta." It can be as simple or elaborate as you wish. You line the plate with lettuce and pile on any of the delicacies you desire.

The traditional selections of antipasto includes: a few slices of salami, prosciutto, slices of cheese, olives, pickled or grilled vegetables. Serve with garlic bread or bread sticks for a delightful gastronomical prelude to a wonderful dinner.

Mushrooms with Sausage

1½ lbs. mushrooms
3 tbsp. olive oil
3 cloves of chopped garlic
½ tsp. salt
¼ tsp. pepper
¼ tsp. oregano
½ lb. sweet sausage
4 tbsp. tomato sauce

Wipe mushrooms clean. Mushrooms should never be washed. Take sausage meat out of casing. Heat oil in skillet and brown sausage. Add mushrooms, garlic, salt, pepper and oregano. Sauté for 1 minute, then add tomato sauce and cook over low heat for 10 minutes, stirring frequently.

Meat Lasagna

1 lb. lasagna
1 lb. chopped meat
1 lb. sweet sausage
2 lb. ricotta cheese
1 lb. mozzarella
1 c. grated cheese

¾ c. bread crumbs
1 egg
3 cloves of garlic
1 small onion
¼ c. parsley
½ c. red wine

3 leaves fresh basil
(*or dried basil*)
2 28 oz. cans
of Italian tomatoes
1 can tomato paste
¼ c. milk

Prepare meat balls first: mix 1 lb. of chopped meat with egg, garlic, parsley, grated cheese and wet bread crumbs. Add salt and pepper to taste. Take a small amount of chopped meat mixture in hand and form a round ball. Brown the meat balls and sausage in a skillet. In a separate pot, sauté olive oil, onion, garlic and basil. Add tomato paste and stir. Add two cans of tomatoes, wine, cook to boil and then add the sausage and meat balls. Cook for approximately 2 hours over low flame. After sauce is done you are now ready to make the lasagna. Boil lasagna in pot according to package directions. When lasagna noodles are cooked, drain water and let the noodle cool.

Coat the bottom of a baking pan with tomato sauce. Arrange cooked lasagna noodles by overlapping the strips to form one layer. Spread ricotta and slice meat balls and sausage onto lasagna noodle. You need not cover entire noodle; there should be spaces between the meat and cheese. Sprinkle chopped mozzarella and grated cheese over top of layer and then add enough sauce to wet the entire layer. Repeat for second layer. Cook at 350 for approximately 30 minutes or until mozzarella is fully melted. Take out of oven and let stand for 20 minutes to set before serving.

Chicken with Potato and Peas

1 frying chicken (cut into 8 pieces)
½ tsp. salt
½ tsp. pepper
4 tbsp. olive oil
1 large onion, sliced
4 potatoes, peeled and quartered
1 can of peas
pinch of paprika

Wash and dry chicken pieces and arrange in baking pan. Place potatoes between the chicken pieces. Sprinkle peas, salt, pepper, paprika and onions over chicken. Drizzle olive oil over entire pan. Bake in oven at 350 degrees for 30 minutes and then turn pieces of chicken over and stir potatoes in juice. Bake for an additional 30 minutes or until chicken and potatoes are tender.

Carciofi

(Stuffed Artichokes)

4 medium artichokes
1 c. bread crumbs
3 cloves of chopped garlic
¼ tsp. salt
⅛ tsp. pepper
¼ tsp. chopped fresh parsley
¼ cup grated cheese
¼ cup extra virgin olive oil
juice of ½ lemon

Remove the artichoke stems, and with a scissor, trim the pointed ends of the leaves. Spread leaves apart and rinse thoroughly. Prepare bread crumb mixture; add bread crumbs, garlic, salt, pepper, parsley, and cheese in a bowl. Pour olive oil and mix with fork until you wet bread crumb mixture. With a small spoon, stuff a small amount of the mixture to each leaf of the artichoke. Arrange the artichokes in upright position in a shallow casserole or deep skillet. Add water — it should reach bottom of chokes enough to steam. Squeeze lemon juice over the top and drizzle each one with olive oil. Cover and simmer over low heat for approximately 45 minutes. Be sure to check and add more water frequently. Artichokes are done when leaf pulls out easily.

Escarole Salad

1 head of escarole,
washed & dried
1 red onion, sliced
Small can black olives
½ c. extra virgin olive oil
½ tsp. salt
Juice of ½ lemon

Cut escarole into pieces and sprinkle salt directly onto salad (this allows the flavor of the escarole to come out). Add olive oil, onions, black olives (may add tomato if desired). Mix well and serve.

Peperoni Imbottiti

4 med. size red peppers
1 egg
½ c. grated cheese
1 can black pitted sliced olives
1 can anchovies
4 cloves chopped garlic
¼ tsp. chopped fresh parsley
1 tbsp. capers
salt and pepper to taste
¼ c. olive oil
1 loaf of hard Italian bread
(*or 1½ c. bread crumbs*)

Core the peppers, rinse and dry. Soak Italian bread in water until soft. Squeeze out excess water. In a skillet, sauté each side of the peppers and put aside, then sauté in oil, anchovies, capers and parsley. Add the bread, olives, salt and pepper to taste stirring constantly until well blended. Take mixture out of skillet and cool in a bowl. When cool, add egg and cheese and mix well. Stuff the peppers. Arrange in baking dish and drizzle oil over them. Bake in oven for approximately 30 minutes or until tender.

Castagne (Roasted Chestnuts)

No meal would be complete unless a tray of roaste chestnuts (castagne) were served. Cut a crisscross in the pointed end of the chestnuts. It is important to cut the "X" in the chestnuts. This allows the steam to escape while cooking or they can explode in the oven. Cover with a little water and bake in oven for approximately 20 to 30 minutes. Serve with fresh fruit and a bowl of mixed nuts.

Momma's Family Lunches

Poppa was in the scrap metal business and attended to his route every day. His two sons helped with the business. Their day started early morning and the boys were reluctant to get out of bed. Momma would sit on the edge of their beds every morning attempting to get them up to start the day. It always took several shakes from her before they would get up.

Momma made her boys lunch every day. Each of her boys sandwiches was made from a full loaf of Italian bread, and ranged from peppers and eggs to assortments of various Italian cold cuts, garnished with vinegar eggplant or roasted peppers. Nowhere could you get a lunch like hers.

Bite into her sandwiches and juices would overflow. Today you could probably feed several people with her one sandwich. Her boys would never starve. She was probably the originator of the six foot hero.

Momma's

HOLIDAY COOKIES AND CAKES

Amaretto Balls

2 c. confectioners' sugar
2 c. chopped walnuts
2 c. chocolate wafers
¾ c. Amaretto

Mash chocolate wafers in blender until smooth. Add sugar, amaretto and 1 cup of walnuts. Roll into little balls. Roll the balls in the remaining chopped walnuts and chill for about ½ hour.

Bows

1½ c. flour	2 c. sugar
½ tsp. salt	3 eggs

2 tsp. vanilla
2 tsp. baking powder
6 tbsp. of sweet butter
4 tsp. water
(*optional: use Anisette instead of water*)

Mix all wet ingredients with flour, salt, sugar and baking powder. Knead well. Dough may be sticky add more flour until dough is dry and smooth. Roll out and cut into 1" x 2" strips then twist in the middle once or twice to form a bow. Deep fry in hot oil for a few minutes until golden brown. Top with confectioners' sugar.

Cinnamon Cookies

Dough:

2½ c. flour
2 tsp. baking powder
2 eggs
½ lb. sweet butter
2 tbsp. sugar
½ pint sour cream

Mix all ingredients well then chill dough for about 1½ hours.

Filling:

1 c. sugar
2 tsp. cinnamon
1 c. chopped walnuts
1 5 oz. box raisins (*optional*)

Roll out dough. Sprinkle cinnamon sugar, nuts and raisins over dough. I find it easier to place dough in a round pizza pan to cut into triangular shapes about 2 inches and about 2½ inches long. Roll up and bake at 350 degrees for about 10 to 15 minutes. Makes about 4 dozen cookies.

Anginetti Cookies

4 c. sifted flour
4 tsp. baking powder
pinch of salt
4 eggs
⅔ c. sugar
½ c. oil
⅔ c. milk
1½ tbsp. vanilla

In a small bowl mix the eggs, sugar, oil, milk and vanilla, mixing well after adding each item. Mix the flour, baking powder and salt, then add the liquid mixture to the dry ingredients. Mix well. If dough seems too loose add a little flour. Take a pinch of dough and roll to about ½-inch thick by 3 inches long. Twirl and roll up like a snake, then bake at 350 degrees for 20 to 25 minutes till lightly browned. Let cool.

ICING: Blend ¾ cup of confectioners' sugar, 1 tsp. of flavoring (either anise extract or lemon extract), add a little milk to make a paste. Dip cookies in icing and let dry. May need a few coats of icing depending how thick you like it coated. Sprinkle nonpareils for color. Let dry on wax paper. Serves approximately 5 dozen cookies.

Coconut Balls

½ c. butter (*1 stick*)
2 c. confectioners' sugar
3 c. flaked coconut
1 tbsp. milk
2 squares (2 oz.) semi sweet
chocolate, melted

Melt butter in a saucepan then remove from heat. Add mild and sugar, mix well. Then add coconut and blend it well into mixture. Shape into rounded balls, about 1 tsp. Make a dent in center of ball. Place on wax lined cookie sheet. Fill centers with melted chocolate mixture. Chill until firm. Store in refrigerator. Also can be frozen.

Cream Cheese Cake

Mix together:
2 lbs. cream cheese
1 pint sour cream
4 eggs

Then add to mixture:
1 tsp. vanilla
1½ c. sugar
4 tbsp. flour

Mix all ingredients until smooth. Pour into spring pan and bake at 350 degrees for 1 hour. Leave cake in oven for another hour with oven off and door open.

Cream Puffs

1 c. water
½ c. oil
1 c. flour
pinch of salt
4 eggs

Bring to a boil the cup of water and ½ cup of oil. Take off stove and add the flour and keep stirring until it comes into a ball. Use a wooden spoon for easier blending. Add 4 eggs and mix until it becomes a thick batter. Butter a cookie sheet. Heat oven to 400 degrees. Drop a heaping teaspoon onto cookie sheet. Bake in 400-degree oven for approximately 15 minutes. When the puff rises, lower to 375 degrees. When puff gets to a light brown take out of oven.

Cream Filling

½ pint of heavy cream
1 box of instant vanilla pudding
½ c. milk

Whip up ½ pint of heavy cream until it becomes thick. Add 1 box of instant vanilla pudding and ½ cup of milk. As you are adding the ingredients keep mixing. Mix until batter gets thick. Split the cooled puffs in half and fill with pudding. Sprinkle with confectioners' sugar. Makes approx. 24 cream puffs.

Macaroon Rum Balls

1 pkg, coconut macaroon mix
¼ cup hot water
1 c. finely chopped nuts
1 tbsp. rum flavoring
Confectioners' sugar or cocoa
Option: *Dip in chocolate & twizzle with white icing*

Mix macaroon mix (dry), water, nuts and rum flavoring. Shape mixture into 1" balls. Roll balls into confectioners' sugar or cocoa. Can store several days in covered container. Makes about 3 dozen.

Pasticiotti

Pastry:
2 c. of all-purpose flour
pinch of salt
½ c. butter
½ c. sugar
2 egg yolks
grated rind of one lemon

Filling:
1½ lb. ricotta
6 tbsp. confectioners' sugar
2 egg yolks
pinch of cinnamon
1 tsp. grated lemon rind

Prepare pastry: sift flour, salt and sugar into a bowl. Cut in butter and with fingertips distribute the butter evenly through the flour. Add egg yolks, one at a time, mixing with a wooden spoon, blend in lemon rind. Work with hand until dough is soft. You may have to add a little water to make a dough consistency. Knead until smooth. Wrap in wax paper and refrigerate for at least one hour. Roll out dough onto a floured board. Cut pastry into rounds to fit into greased muffin pan. You could use a large glass to get even cuts of dough. Save some dough for the top of the pastry.

Filling: Combine ricotta with the rest of ingredients; mix well. Fill prepared pastry section. Cut leftover pastry into small strips and place strips crisscross over filling. Trim edges. Bake in moderate 350 degrees oven for 40 to 50 minutes. Cool in oven. Makes 8 to 10 pastries.

Pizza Dolce
(Italian Cheese Cake)

Cheesecake Pastry:

¾ c. all-purpose flour
⅓ c. margarine or butter, softened
2 tbsp. sugar
⅛ tsp. salt

Mix all ingredients until blended. Rollout dough to cover bottom of pan. Press evenly in bottom of greased spring form pan, 9x3". Bake 5 minutes.

Cheesecake Filling:

1½ lbs. ricotta cheese
½ c. sugar
3 tbsp. all-purpose flour
1 tsp. grated orange peel
1 tsp. vanilla
¼ tsp. salt
3 eggs
2 tbsp. finely chopped candied citron
2 tbsp. powered sugar
½ tsp. ground cinnamon

Heat oven to 475 degrees. Prepare cheesecake filling. Reduce oven temperature to 350 degrees. Beat cheese, sugar, flour, orange peel, vanilla, salt and eggs on high speed about 4 minutes. Mix in candied citron. Pour mixture over baked pastry. Bake for 1¼ to 1½ hours or until center is set and top is golden brown. Cool for 15 minutes. Refrigerate at least 12 hours, then run metal spatula along side of cheesecake to loosen. Mix powered sugar and cinnamon and sprinkle over top of cake.

Pignoli Cookies

1 c. (5 oz.) pignoli nuts
1 can (8 oz.) or 1 roll
(7 oz.) almond paste
½ c. granulated sugar
1 tbsp. all-purpose flour
2 egg whites
1 tsp. fresh grated lemon peel

Heat over to 400 degrees. Line cookie sheet with parchment paper or you can use a brown paper bag. In a medium bowl; beat the almond paste, sugar, flour, egg whites and lemon peel with an electric mixer until smooth. Wet hands and form dough into 1 inch balls, using a heaping teaspoon for each ball. Press ball into pignoli nuts, flattening slightly and coating on one side only. Place nut side up about 1 inch apart on cookie sheet.

Bake 8 to 10 minutes until tops feel firm and dry when lightly pressed. Cool completely on cookie sheet. Peel off lining.

Sesame Cookies

1¼ lbs. all-purpose flour
½ lb. confectioners' sugar
1½ tbsp. baking powder
½ lb. Crisco shortening
1 tbsp. vanilla
6 eggs
1 12 oz. bag of sesame seeds

Mix all dry ingredients together; then add 3 eggs and vanilla and mix well. Add Crisco to the dough and knead well. Take small pinches of dough (about the size of a quarter) and roll into a log shape.

Beat 3 eggs in a bowl. Dip cookie dough in egg batter. Then in a separate dish roll dough in sesame seeds. Bake until cookies get brown, about 20 to 25 minutes at 400 degrees. Makes approximately 120 cookies.

Sugar Cookies

2 lbs. all-purpose flour
1 lb. sugar
5 tsp. baking powder
1 tsp. vanilla
6 eggs
1 lb. Crisco shortening

Mix all dry ingredients. Mix eggs and vanilla then add to dry mixture and mix well. Knead dough well. Roll flat then cut with cookie cutters. Bake on ungreased cookie sheets for 7 to 10 minutes at 350 degrees.

Struffoli

(Honey Balls)

2 lbs. all-purpose flour
10 eggs
1 c. sugar
1 tbsp. baking powder
1 shot glass anisette liquor
½ lb. softened margarine
1 large jar of honey
¼ c. orange peel
¼ c. nonpareil
colored sprinkles

Flour conversion: *3 3/4 cups = 1 lb.*

Momma used to mix all her ingredients right on the counter top. I used the kitchen aide mixer which is much easier. Mix all dry ingredients. Then mix the eggs and anisette together, and pour mixture into the flour. Add margarine and knead dough well. Cut dough into small sections and roll into long strips about ½-inch wide and 12 inches long. Sprinkle flour to dough to eliminate being sticky. Cut into small pieces of about ¼-inch and roll into ball. Deep fry until golden brown. Keep balls in a large bowl until they are cooled.

In a large pot, pour honey and orange peel and heat over low flame until the honey is thin. Once honey is heated it becomes easier to work with. Remove pot from the stove and add balls into honey mixture stirring continuously until all the balls are covered with the honey mixture. Place honey balls in plates and sprinkle confetti over the top to add color (can add slivered almonds if desired).

Tiramisu

4 egg yolks
½ c. sugar
½ c. milk
1 lb. ricotta cheese
2 oz. semisweet chocolate (grated)
2 c. heavy cream
2 tbsp. cocoa
½ c. cold espresso coffee
2 tbsp. Tia Maria liquor (*optional: use rum*)
24 ladyfinger cookies (*optional: Italian Savoiardi cookies*)

Beat egg yolks and sugar in a saucepan on medium speed about 30 seconds or until well blended. Beat in milk. Heat to boiling over medium heat, stirring constantly. Reduce heat to low. Boil and stir 1 minute; remove from heat. Place plastic wrap or waxed paper directly onto milk mixture in saucepan. Refrigerate about 2 hours or until cool.

Mix milk mixture, cheese and chocolate. Beat heavy cream and 2 tbsp. cocoa in chilled medium bowl until stiff. Mix espresso and Tia Maria liquor.

Dip half of the ladyfingers in espresso mixture (do not soak). Arrange in single layer in ungreased square baking dish, 8x8x2." Spread half of the whipped cream mixture. Cover and refrigerate at least 3 hours. Sprinkle with cocoa.

Walnut Cups

2 c. flour
6 oz. cream cheese
2 sticks butter (*softened*)

Mix all above ingredients then roll into small balls. Press and shape dough into mini cupcake pan.

Filling:

1 c. chopped walnuts
1 c. chopped almonds
2 eggs
4 tbsp. vanilla
4 tbsp. melted butter
2 c. brown sugar

Mix all ingredients: fill cups half way with filling. Bake at 350 degrees for 20 minutes. Makes approximately 60 cups.

Zeppole

1¼ c. flour
1 package active dry yeast
⅛ tsp. sugar
1 c. warm water
⅛ tsp. salt
1½ c. vegetable oil

Dissolve yeast, salt and sugar in warm water. Stir in flour and mix well. Cover with a dishtowel and let dough rise in a warm area for approximately 1½ hours or until dough doubles in size. Heat oil. Drop a tablespoon of dough into oil and fry until golden brown. Cool and then add confectioners' sugar before serving.

Cannoli

Shells:

2 c. flour
1 tbsp. sugar
¼ tsp. salt
2 tbsp. shortening
¾ c. Marsala or red wine, dry white wine
1 egg white
metal tubes for cannoli shells

Combine flour, shortening, sugar and salt. While kneading mixture, add the wine into the dough until it forms into a ball. Mixture may be coarse; add a little more wine until dough is smooth. Cover with a cloth and let stand for one hour. Cut the dough into four quarters mad roll into a thin sheet about ¼-inch thick. Cut dough into 4 inch squares. Place metal tube diagonally across each square wrapping dough around tube. Overlap ends and seal with egg white. Flare out end of dough to form opening. Heat oil in a large deep fryer. Drop one or two tubes into hot oil and fry for about 2 to 3 minutes or until dough become golden brown. Remove from pan and let cool. Then gently slide out tube from shell.

Filling:

2 c. of whole milk ricotta cheese
½ c. confectioners' sugar
¼ tsp. cinnamon
¼ c. heavy cream
½ tsp. vanilla
¼ c. small semisweet chocolate chips
(*optional: tsp. chopped pistachio nuts*)

Mix ricotta with all dry ingredients. In a separate bowl beat heavy cream until stiff. Fold cream into ricotta mixture. Stir in chocolate chips and (or) citron. If mixture has excess liquid, drain in a strainer before filling. Fill cannoli shells when you are ready to serve. That will avoid them getting soggy. Garnish with confectioner sugar.

Momma's Sunday Best

Sunday afternoons were always reserved for dinner at Momma's house. The entire family, would gather around her large oak dining room table and engage in vigorous conversation. We caught up with the weeks gossip, continued old arguments and even discovered new ones. God forbid if one family member was missing, you knew they would be the target of conversation. However, it should be made clear, this was only allowed within the family. Heaven forbid an outsider was caught gossiping about a family member. The family always stood up for and protected one another. To this day it is still understood, you can always depend upon your family.

Momma's Sunday dinner started in the mid-afternoon and lasted well into the evening. The Sunday meal would consist of a small antipasto (usually celery and olives), a pasta dish, preceded by one or more main dishes of meat and or poultry, served with several side dishes of vegetables. Momma would then bring out the fruit and nuts. My fondest memory was that of her beautiful lace table cloth, imported from her native Naples, completely covered with nut shells.

There was never any fuss made over the untidiness of the table. Momma had it under control and had it cleaned up without ever disturbing anyone's conversation. She then served the black coffee and pastries. La Machinetta is the coffee pot used to make black coffee. Momma always served the black coffee on a tray along with a bottle of anisette and lemon rind. Those espresso cups had a way of making the most noise at the table, since the spoon stirring the contents couldn't help hitting the sides of the cup. It was a symphony of clanging noise. It marked the end of the meal and was to help you digest. By this time it was well into the evening and one would think that dinner was over. Wrong. Momma would then announce with a twinkle in her eye "nu pezza di sandwich" for the ride home just in case you got hungry. As I look back at those dinners, they were wonderful times spent with the family, and I miss them very much.

Momma's
HOT APPETIZERS

Potato Croquettes

6 lg. potatoes
3 lg. eggs separated
1 c. grated cheese
(Parmigano-Reggiano)
2 tbsp. of chopped Italian parsley
2 c. seasoned bread crumbs
salt and pepper to taste
vegetable oil for frying

Boil the potatoes until tender. Remove from pot and mash. Set aside and let cool. When potatoes are cool add egg yolks, cheese, parsley, salt and pepper.

Mix mixture well. Form potato mixture into log shapes. In a shallow dish beat the egg whites until they become frothy. Dip potato logs into egg whites and then roll them in the bread crumbs. Place potato logs on a wire rack and dry for about 15 minutes.

Pour about ½-inch of vegetable oil into frying pan and heat over medium heat. Drop potato log into pan turning log to fry until golden brown. Remove and place log on paper towel to absorb excess oil. Serve hot.

Stuffed Mushrooms

30 mushrooms
½ lb. sausage (take off casing)
1 c. shredded mozzarella
1 c. seasoned bread crumbs
1 tbsp chopped Italian parsley
½ c. grated cheese
2 tbsp. butter
2 cloves chopped garlic
salt and pepper to taste

Chop the mushroom stems and brown in butter, add garlic. Once browned put in bowl then brown the sausage meat. Combine both mixtures and let cool. Once cooled, add mozzarella, bread crumbs, parsley and cheese. Stuff mushroom caps. Place into a grease cooking sheet and sprinkle with a little love oil. Bake for approximately 20 minutes.

Zucchini Frittata

2 lg. chopped zucchini
2 cloves chopped garlic
1 tbsp. chopped basil
½ cup grated cheese
6 eggs
salt and pepper to taste
vegetable oil for frying

In a large frying pan, sauté garlic and zucchini. In a bowl, beat the eggs, basil and cheese. Add to pan. Salt and pepper to taste. Fry on one side until bottom is firm. Take pan off top of the stove and place in oven to broil top until done. You should be able to remove from pan in a perfect round frittata.

Stuffed Arancini

(Rice Balls)

2 c. of Arborio Rice
4 eggs
2 c. grated cheese

4 c. water
or 32 oz. of chicken stock
flour for dredging
2 c. Italian seasoned bread crumbs

For Dredging;
2 beaten eggs
2 beaten egg whites

Stuffing:
1/2 lb. chopped meat
1 clove chopped garlic
15 oz. can tomato sauce
small can of sweet peas
1 onion
7 oz. bag of shredded mozzarella

Cook rice the night before, drain and refrigerate. This allows the rice to be sticky and will form a ball. Make the stuffing: Chop onion and sauté until onion becomes caramelized. Add the garlic. Cook until garlic becomes soft. Do not overcook garlic. Add chopped meat and let it brown. Add tomato sauce and peas. Cook over low heat for approximately 15 minutes. In a large bowl beat the 4 eggs and cheese together. Then add the rice and mix well. Take a small amount of rice mixture in your hand and form rice into a cup. Add about a teaspoon of stuffing mixture and a pinch of mozzarella. Add more rice around mixture to form a ball. Prepare pot for frying (add oil and heat). Dredge ball in flour. Shake off excess flour and dip into beaten egg mixture. Coat all with egg mixture then dredge in bread crumbs. Roll ball until bread crumbs are evenly coated. Immediately roll ball in egg whites. Drop in pot to fry. Fry until ball becomes golden brown.

Caponata

4 med. eggplants
2 cloves diced garlic
1½ c. olive oil
4 sliced onions
½ c. tomato sauce
4 stalks diced celery
pinch of oregano
½ c. capers
12 green olives, pitted & cut into pieces
1 tbsp. pine nuts
½ c. wine vinegar
¼ c. sugar
salt and pepper to taste
(*optional: ¼ c. sugar*)

Peel and dice eggplant. Fry in 1 cup hot olive oil. Remove fried eggplant from skillet. Add remain oil and add onions. Fry until onions get soft then add garlic until garlic gets soft. Add tomato sauce and celery, cook until celery is tender, adding a little water if necessary. Add oregano, capers, olives and pine nuts and fried eggplant. Heat vinegar in a small saucepan and dissolve sugar in the vinegar. Add vinegar over eggplant and simmer for approximately 20 minites. Let it cool. This will keep in the refrigerator for a long time.

Momma's
Delicious Soups

Pasta Fagiole

1 15 oz. can of Great Northern White Beans
1 14 oz. can of tomatoes
2 tbsp. olive oil
2 cloves chopped garlic
1 8 oz. can chicken stock
small piece pancetta, chopped
8 oz. shell or elbow macaroni
pinch oregano
pinch red pepper
salt, pepper to taste
grated cheese

In saucepan sauté pancetta until soft. Add garlic. Add chicken stock, tomatoes, white beans, oregano, red pepper, salt and pepper to taste. *Optional: add string beans, celery, escarole or swiss chard.* Cook for about ½ hour. Add elbow macaroni and cook until done. Serve with grated cheese.

Split Pea & Ham Soup

2 tablespoons olive oil
32 oz. container chicken stock
1 large chopped onion
2 stalks chopped celery
2 chopped carrots
3 cloves chopped garlic
1 lb. green split peas
1 ham bone
croutons
salt and pepper to taste

In a large saucepan heat the olive oil. Add the onion, carrots, celery and sauté until vegetables are soft. Add garlic and cook until soft. Add split peas, chicken stock and ham bone, salt and pepper. Cover and simmer for about 1 hour. Remove ham bone from soup and pull ham off the bone. Add meat back to soup Serve and top with croutons.

Potato Soup with Sausage

1 medium onion, thinly sliced
1½ lbs. Yukon gold potatoes
½ lb. Italian sausage (2 links)
48 oz. container chicken broth
½ tsp. parsley
½ tsp. salt
3 tbsp. butter
½ c. heavy cream

Cut potatoes into thin slices. Remove casing from sausage. In a large saucepan, place sausage in pot and crumble, breaking apart with a wooden spoon. Stir in onions and cook for about 2 minutes until onions become soft. Stir in potatoes, chicken broth, salt and pepper. Cover and cook until potatoes become tender. Then puree soup and stir in heavy cream add parsley to top. Serve.

Tortellini Spinach Soup

9 oz. package cheese tortellini
1 pkg. fresh spinach
32 oz. container of chicken stock
1 tbsp. olive oil
2 cloves chopped garlic
½ chopped carrot
small can white beans
small can stewed tomatoes
1 tbsp. grated cheese
salt and pepper to taste

In a large saucepan, heat the olive oil and add garlic. Cook garlic until soft, add spinach, carrot, beans and chicken stock. Cover and simmer for about 5 minutes. Add tortellini cook until tortellini is done. Serve in dish and sprinkle top with grated cheese.

Escarole Soup with Meat Balls

(Italian Wedding Soup)

1 head escarole
2 32 oz containers chicken broth
2 carrots chopped
salt and pepper to taste
½ lb. of ditalini

Meat Balls:
½ lb. chopped beef or veal
1 egg
1 clove chopped garlic
½ c. seasoned bread crumbs
½ c. grated cheese
(*preferably Parmigiano - Reggiano*)
pinch parsley
salt and pepper

Cut the escarole stems and wash escarole well. Stack the escarole leaves and cut into strips. In a large saucepan, combine escarole, carrots and chicken broth. Cover and simmer for about 20 minutes or until escarole is tender. Mix together all ingredients for the meat balls. Shape into tiny balls. When the escarole is cooked, drop the meat balls and pasta into soup and simmer for another 20 minutes. Salt and pepper to taste. Serve hot and sprinkle soup with grated cheese.

Momma Prepares for Her Sunday Best

Sunday mornings, Momma would get up early in order to prepare her sauce for the macaroni. It wouldn't be considered a Sunday unless we had macaroni. Her kitchen always gave the appearance of being sparkling clean. She loved her double kitchen window with the white priscilla curtains. The cabinets were wood with a high gloss; the stove was white porcelain; counter tops were shining white with everything arranged in proper order. The table was chrome with a white top that always sparkled.

She would fry those meat balls in a heavy cast iron fry pan. The aroma of meatballs frying would make her children sneak in the kitchen and steal a few before they were put into the sauce.

Nothing tastes better than newly fried meatballs and crisp Italian bread dipped in sauce. When she caught them snacking on the food she was preparing, she would shout out, "Son of a gun, getta outa here!" and proceed to chase them with the wooden spoon. That famous wooden spoon was the source of her authority. When Momma ran after you with the wooden spoon, you knew she meant what she was saying.

I remember one Christmas when Momma changed her recipe for lasagna. It was the year I was pregnant with my second child. The smell of meat made me violently sick, much less would I eat it. Momma made her lasagna without meat especially for me. Everyone was upset that she altered her recipe. Her son said to her in a bewildered voice, "Mom, what the hell is this?" She replied in her broken English, "Eh (as her shoulders would shrug, her eyes looking at me and her fingers pointing to my belly) sheda gotta eat, sheda eata for two." No one ever disputed that gesture.

Momma's
Meat & Fish Dishes

Flank Steak Oregnata

1 2 lb. flank steak
2 onions chopped
½ c. white wine
1 lemon
1 tsp. chopped garlic
1 tbsp. oregano
pinch of sage
1 tsp parsley
1 can 15 oz. plum tomatoes
¼ c. olive oil

Soak overnight in refrigerator; flank steak, onions, lemon and white wine. Next day remove from marinade and keep half onions. Roll out flank steak and pound with garlic. Place in roasting pan. Cover meat with half onion mixture add cut in quarters tomatoes, sage, parley and oregano. Sprinkle with olive oil. Cover with foil and bake in 350 degree oven until steak is tender approximately 1 hour or depending on thickness of the steak.

Stuffed Chicken Breast with Marsala

4 chicken breasts
½ pkg. of frozen chopped spinach *drained*
1 egg
1 large onion chopped
½ lb. sausage meat
¼ c. grated cheese
1 tsp. chopped garlic
1 c. flour
¼ c. Marsala
½ c. chicken stock
½ stick butter

Butterfly chicken breast and pound to make ready for stuffing. Sauteé onions, garlic. Add sausage and chopped spinach. Remove from heat and slightly cool. Add egg and grated cheese. Mix mixture well. Stuff chicken breast and roll. You can stick toothpick in roll to hold securely. Roll stuffed chicken breast in flour and fry in pan until all sides of chicken is braised. Add chicken stock and marsala and cook for approx. 10 minutes. Add cold butter to pan and roll around. Cover and cook for 10 minutes.

Annie's Pork Chops with Sweet Vinegar Peppers

4 loin pork chops (*thick cut*)
1 egg
1 c. Italian seasoned bread crumbs
1 c. panko bread crumbs
1 jar sweet vinegar peppers
red & green peppers
olive oil
pinch of salt and pepper

Sprinkle salt on pork chops. Beat 1 egg and dip chop into mixture. Combine seasoned bread crumbs and panko crumbs. Dip pork chops on both sides. In fry pan brown on both sides. Set oven temperature at 400 degrees. Put pork chops in baking pan and bake for 45 minutes. Then add jar of sweet peppers (cut) with the juice over the chops. Bake another 10 minutes.

Honey BBQ Baked Brisket

1 beef brisket 3-3½ lbs.
⅓ c. honey
½ tsp. garlic powder
1 envelope Lipton onion soup mix
½ c. BBQ sauce
¼ c. ketchup

Mix honey, garlic powder, Lipton soup mix, BBQ sauce and ketchup until blended. Line roasting pan with heavy aluminum foil with enough to hang over pan. Place brisket in pan and pour mixture over it. Fold aluminum wrap and seal brisket, leaving a small open air space. Bake at 325 degrees for 3–3½ hours.

Pork Roast with Sauerkraut

3-4 lb. pork loin
4 potatoes
1 medium onion
27 oz. can of sauerkraut
6 oz. beer
1 tsp. fennel seeds
⅛ c. oil
salt & pepper

Use a dutch over fryer to cook on top of stove.

Brown the onions and potatoes until the potatoes have a crispy crust. Add salt and pepper to taste. Remove from pan. Place pork loin in pan and brown on all sides. Add the sauerkraut, with the juices. Cook on low heat for 45 minutes. Then add the beer and fennel seeds. Cover and simmer for approximately another 45 minutes or until pork is done.

Steak Pizzaiola

2 lbs. chuck steak *thick cut*
1 28 oz. can crushed tomatoes
1 tsp. chopped garlic
½ tsp. oregano
fresh parsley
or 1 tsp. dried parsley
¼ tsp. salt
¼ tsp. black pepper
1 green pepper chopped
½ lb. mushrooms
½ c. red wine

Trim meat of all visible fat. Broil steak in oven on both sides until meat is braised. Remove from oven and set oven at 350 degrees. Pour tomatoes and wine over meat and add salt, pepper, parsley garlic, oregano. Cover with foil and cook for approx. 1 hour. Then add peppers and mushrooms and cook for an additional ½ hour or until meat is tenderIn addition, you instead of baking in oven you can cook in a covered pan on stove top.

Osso Buocco

2 veal shanks *about 2 inches thick*
3 to 4 tbsp. olive oil
1 finely chopped onion
1 finely chopped carrot
1 finely chopped stalk celery
2 cloves chopped garlic
1 tbsp. parsley
1 tsp. lemon juice
¼ c. white wine
½ c. chicken stock
1 c. chopped tomato or 8 oz. can of tomato sauce
¼ c. flour for dredging

Salt both side of veal shank and dredge in flour to coat both side. Heat oil in saucepan and add veal shanks. Brown on both sides then remove from pan. Add onions, carrot, celery and sauté until vegetable gets soft. Add garlic and tomatoes. Scrape bottom with wooden spoon to get the flavor on the vegetables. Add the veal back to saucepan and add the chicken stock, wine, parsley and lemon juice. Cover pan and simmer for about 1 hour or until veal is tender.

Minestra with Pork

1 head savoy cabbage, chopped
1 lb. spare ribs
2 tbsp. olive oil
3 cloves of garlic, chopped
1 32 oz. carton chicken stock
red pepper
salt and pepper to taste

In a large saucepan, brown the spare ribs in olive oil. Add garlic and sauté. When garlic becomes soft (do not brown garlic), add the cabbage, chicken stock, red pepper, salt and pepper. Cook until cabbage is done.

Added note: *Momma would serve the cabbage over hard cut up italian bread (**Minestra con Pane**). Sometimes instead of using spare ribs she would use pickled pigs feet.*

Mediterranean Fish

4 5 oz. fish filets
(*flounder, cod, or snapper*)
small onion
2 cloves diced garlic
1 fresh tomato chopped
8 oz. can tomato sauce
pinch of oregano (*fresh if possible*)
½ c. green olives
¼ c. capers
¼ c. dry white wine
(*pinch of red pepper flakes optional*)

Lightly flour fish and brown the filets over medium heat. Remove from pan and set aside. Add onions to same pan and cook until onions get soft, add garlic and the fresh tomato. Cook for a few minutes, then add the can of tomato sauce, oregano, wine and salt and pepper to taste. Cook on low heat for about 10 minutes. Then add fish, olives and capers. Cook for about another 5 minutes or until fish if fully cooked. Serve over rice.

Momma's Neighborhood

Momma and Poppa lived at 306 East 108th St. between Second and Third Avenue in East Harlem. I have been told the apartment was a railroad flat. All the rooms were in direct line of each other. They did not have heat in the apartment as we now have today; they had a coal stove. At that time the community was predominately an Italian neighborhood. Since Momma had no family in America, her friends were considered family. They were her Compares and Commares (Godfathers and Godmothers). They baptized and confirmed each other's children and were considered to be like parents. They were held with great respect in the family circle. They shared their lives and hardships, and helped raise one another's children.

It was a close-knit group and each depended upon the other as family members usually do.

Sundays were special days in their lives. A day put aside for family. Often the Commare and Compare, along with their children, visited and shared Sunday's dinner. The women would cook something special and always shared recipes. Of course they were expressed verbally, since they could not read or write. It was also an era when cousins grew up knowing one another.

They shared their life experiences and formed special bonds. It was an era when families found the time to be together, regardless of how many people they cramped into their kitchens and living rooms. They shared and helped each other get through and enjoy their lives.

Momma's
FAVORITE PASTAS

ORGANIC
RAPINI
$3.00/bu.

Broccoli Rabe with Meat Sauce

1 lb. chopped meat
1 egg
2 tsp. chopped garlic
¼ c. grated cheese
¼ c. bread crumbs
¼ tsp. salt
¼ tsp. pepper
1 bunch broccoli rabe (*rapini*)
1 28 oz. canned tomatoes
4 leaves of fresh basil
 (*can substitute dried*)
pinch of red pepper

Skin the stems to make them tender. Wash and then chop. Set aside. Mix chopped meat with egg, 1 tsp. chopped garlic, bread crumbs, grated cheese, salt, pepper and red pepper (*can add more red pepper if desired*). In large fry pan brown chopped meat and mash until chopped meat is loose. Add additional tsp. of garlic and tomatoes. Cook for 20 minutes. Add the broccoli rabe. Cook until tender. Serve over penne.

Spaghetti with Crab Sauce

1 large onion chopped
1 tsp. chopped garlic
1 6 oz. can tomato paste
1 28 oz. can tomatoes
fresh sprigs oregano
pinch of red pepper
¼ tsp. salt
¼ tsp. pepper ***(missing crab qty.)***

Prepare live blue crabs. In kitchen sink stun live crabs with hot water. Open top shell and clean out crab.

In large fry pan add olive oil and onions. Sauté onions, add garlic and red pepper. Add can of tomato paste and mix well. Then add 28 oz. can of tomatoes and cook for about 20 minutes. Add crabs and cook for an additional 10 minutes. Serve over spaghetti.

Linguine with Peas & Shrimp

1 lb. large shrimp
1 pint heavy cream
1 can peas
4 tbsp. grated cheese
1 large chopped onion
pinch of salt and pepper
olive oil

In large fry pan sautee`onion in olive oil. Add peas, cream salt and pepper. Mix well. Add shrimp to mixture and cook until shrimp are cooked (turns pink). Add grated cheese and mix. Serve over linguine.

Manicotti

Shells:

3 c. flour
1½ c. water
6 eggs
½ tsp. salt

Beat eggs then add flour, water, salt. Mix well (should look like a pancake batter). Use a 8" fry pan and spray pan with cooking spray. Cook until firm and then flip like a pancake. Makes about 30 shells. Place between wax paper.

Filling:

1½ lbs. ricotta
½ c. grated cheese
t tbsp. parsley
1 egg

Mix all ingredients. Lay out shells flat and with a teaspoon scoop ricotta onto shell and roll so that the shell overlaps and holds filling. Place in baking pan and add sauce. Bake for approximately ½ hour.

Spaghetti con le Sarde

(Sardines)

2 3.5oz. cans sardines in oil
1 stalk chopped celery
½ chopped fennel
1 chopped onion
½ c. calamata or green olives
3 tbsp. pine nuts
salt and pepper to taste
1 16 oz. can tomatoes
1 lb. spaghetti

In saucepan, add the sardine oil (*add additional olive oil if necessary*). Add celery, fennel, onion and sauté over medium heat until vegetables become soft. Add chopped sardines and cook for 3 to 4 minutes. Add the tomatoes, olives and pine nuts. Cover and simmer for about 15 minutes until sauce is done.

Boil spaghetti as per package instructions. Drain and pour sauce over spaghetti.

Bucatini Bolognese

¾ lb. chopped veal
¾ lb. chopped pork
¾ lb.. chopped beef
1 finely chopped onion
1 finely chopped carrot
1 finely chopped celery stalk
2 finely chopped cloves of garlic
28 oz. can tomatoes
small piece of rind of a piece of Parmigano-Reggiano
6 oz. can tomato paste
1 c. chicken broth
½ c.red wine
3 to 4 tbsp. olive oil
1 lb. Bucatini
salt and pepper to taste

In a large bowl mix all the meat together. In a saucepan heat olive oil and add meat mixture. Break up the meat with a wooden spoon while cooking until the meat is browned and crumbly. Remove the meat with a slotted spoon to keep the juices in pan. Set meat aside. Add to saucepan the onion, carrot, celery and garlic until vegetables become soft. Add tomato paste and sauté with vegetable mixture. Cook for about 3 minutes. Add the 28 oz. can of tomatoes. Blend together and simmer for another 3-4 minutes. Add the chicken broth, meat and wine, rind and stir. Salt and pepper to taste and simmer for about an hour. Stir as needed.

Boil bucatini as per package instructions. Drain and place in platter, pour sauce over Bucatini.

Penne ala Vodka

¼ c. olive oil
3 chopped garlic cloves
1 chopped onion
28 oz. can tomatoes
¼ c. vodka
1 c. heavy cream
pinch of red pepper
1 tbsp. chopped parsley
salt and pepper to taste
1 lb. penne

Combine oil, onions and red pepper, parsley,salt and pepper in large skillet and sauté until onions are soft, add garlic and cook until garlic becomes golden but not brown. Blend in tomatoes and simmer uncovered until sauce thickens.

Boil penne as per package instructions. Drain and add to sauce and toss. Add vodka and cream and toss again until all is mixed and serve.

Pasta with Broccoli

1 bunch broccoli florets
2 tbsp.olive oil
1 8 oz. can chicken stock
3 cloves garlic, chopped
pinch of red pepper
¼ c. toasted bread crumbs
salt and pepper to taste
grated cheese
8 oz. penne

In a large saucepan, sauté garlic in olive oil. Add broccoli florets, salt and pepper, red pepper and can of chicken stock. Cook until broccoli is done. Add grated cheese to taste. Cook spaghetti and drain. Pour broccoli in ziti or spaghetti. In individual dishes, sprinkle toasted bread crumbs and additional grated cheese on top.

Pasta é Lenticche

2 32 oz. cartons chicken stock
2 tbsp. olive oil
3 cloves minced garlic
small piece pancetta
  or prosciutto
1 medium chopped onion
2 stalks of celery, chopped
2 carrots, chopped
2 bay leaves
1 16 oz. package of lentils
salt and pepper to taste
8 oz. Ditalini
grated cheese, preferably
  Parmigano-Reggiano

In a saucepan, pour in olive oil and brown the pancetta. When pancetta becomes soft, remove from pan. Add onions and cook for a few minutes. Add garlic, celery, carrots, salt and pepper and cook for a few minutes. Add the pancetta back into pot. Pour in 2 cartons of chicken stock. Add the dry lentils. Stir in by leaves. Simmer for approximately one hour or until the lentils are soft. Cook the pasta as per package instructions. Drain and add to the soup. Sprinkle grated cheese on top.

Lisa's Farfalle with Cauliflower

1 bunch of cauliflower, cut up
2 tbsp. olive oil
2 cloves chopped garlic
1 8 oz. can chicken stock
1 c. dry white wine
8 oz. goat cheese
red pepper
salt and pepper to taste
8 oz. Farfalle pasta
(*shaped like bow ties*)
(*optional: any pasta can be used*)

In a saucepan, sauté garlic in olive oil. Add cauliflower and cook until cauliflower is soft. Add chicken stock, white wine, red pepper, salt and pepper and simmer for a few minutes. Add goat cheese and cook until goat cheese melts into mixture.

Momma's
Classic Desserts

Anisette Toast

2 c. flour
2 tsp. baking powder
pinch of salt
1 c. sugar
½ c. vegetable shortening
4 eggs
⅓ c. anisette

Preheat over to 350 degrees. Grease and flour a 9x12" baking pan. Set aside. Sift together the flour, baking powder and salt. In a separate bowl, cream the sugar and shortening. Then add the eggs one at a time and the anisette. Mix well. The batter will be heavy and will need to smooth out with a spatula.
Bake for approximately 20 minutes or until golden brown.

Cut loaf on a diagonal in strips of ¾-inch thick. Cut the longer strips in half. Place on a flat wire rack and return to oven until toasted.

Biscotti

3½ c. flour
3 eggs
1 c. sugar
2 tsp. baking powder
½ c. vegetable oil
1 tsp. vanilla
¼ tsp. salt
½ c. raisins
1 c. chopped almonds

Plump raisins in boiling water for a few minutes, drain and let cool. Blend eggs with oil. Add the sugar and vanilla until creamy. Add the rest of the ingredients and mix until all is blended. The dough is a very thick dough. Roll dough into 4 long loaves and wrap with wax paper. Place in refrigerator for one hour.

Preheat oven to 350 degrees. Remove wax paper and slice diagonally with a sharp knife into ¾-inch slices. Place slices on a cookie sheet and bake for 15 to 20 minutes or until the top becomes a golden brown. Then turn biscotti and bake for another 15 to 20 minutes or until it becomes golden brown.

Continental Tea Ring

2 c. flour
¼ lb. sweet butter
1 c. sugar
4 eggs slightly beaten
1 c. sour cream
1 tsp. baking soda
1 tsp. baking powder
½ tsp. salt
1 tsp. vanilla

Topping:

1 tsp. cinnamon
¾ c. sugar
¼ c. chopped walnuts and raisins

Preheat oven to 350 degrees.

Grease a tube-type pan (*can use a bundt pan*).

Cream the butter and sugar the add slightly beaten eggs and mix well. Add the baking soda to the sour cream and mix into the batter. Add all the rest of the dry ingredients. Slowly add the vanilla. Put half the batter in tube pan. Sprinkle half of the topping on top of batter and swirl with a knife. Add the remaining batter on top. Add the rest of the topping on top and bake for about 50 minutes to one hour.

Ice Box Cake

1 5 oz. pkg. Jello cook-and-serve chocolate pudding
1 5 oz. pkg. Jello cook-and-serve vanilla pudding
1 box graham crackers
4 c. heavy whipping cream
⅛ tsp. vanilla
pinch of sugar
1 can sliced peaches

Line a 7" x 11" pan with a layer of graham crackers.

Cook chocolate pudding according to package instructions. Pour chocolate pudding onto the graham crackers. Add another layer of graham crackers onto of the pudding mixture. Cook vanilla pudding according to package instructions and add onto graham cracker making two layers of pudding, Add another layer of graham crackers onto the vanilla pudding. Let it cool.

In a bowl pour whipping cream, vanilla, and sugar. Beat until cream become whip cream. Pour onto of cake and smooth cream evenly over cake. Decorate top with sliced peaches. Refrigerate until pudding is cold.

Momma alway made the cake for her children's Birthday. It was always a favorite.

HAPPY BIRTHD

Pastiera di Grano

(Easter Wheat Pie)

Pie Crust:

2 c. sifted flour
½ c. sugar
pinch of salt
¼ c. butter
3 egg yolks
1 tbsp. mild

Mix flour, salt and sugar. Cut in butter evenly through flour mixture. Stir in egg yolks one at a time. Work until dough is manageable. Add milk. Turn onto a lightly floured board and knead until smooth. Form into a ball and chill for 30 minutes. Divide the ball in half, roll on lightly floured board to about ⅛-inch thick (large enough to line a deep 10" pie plate). Butter pie plate and line with pastry, leaving ½-inch overhang. Roll out other piece of dough and cut into ¾-inch strips for lattice topping.

Filling:

1 can wheat
¼ c. milk, scalded
¼ tsp. salt
¼ tsp. sugar
¼ c. citron, diced
¼ orange peel, diced
1½ lbs. ricotta
1 c. sugar
6 eggs, separated
1 tbsp. orange water
1 tsp. vanilla
2 tbsp. confectioners' sugar

In the scalded milk, mix wheat, salt and sugar. Boil for 5 minutes. Remove from heat, add citron and orange peel, set aside. To prepare filling, beat ricotta and sugar, then add egg yolks, vanilla and orange water, blend well. Stir in prepared wheat and fold in beaten egg whites.

Pour into pie shell. Arrange lattice topping over filling, flute edge. Bake in preheated 350 degrees oven for 1 hour or until firm in center Let cool in oven with door open. Refrigerate. To serve sprinkle with confectioners' sugar.

For your information: wheat can be purchased by the ounce in an Italian specialty market. For this recipe use 2½ ounces or ½ cup. Simmer grain with 1 cup water and the peeled rind of one orange for 30 to 35 minutes.

Pizza Rustica

Easter Meat Pie

1 dz. eggs
2 lbs. ricotta
½ c. grating cheese
½ tsp. black pepper
1 sweet hard sausage, sliced
1 lb. pepperoni, sliced
¾ lb. sweet prosciutto
½ lb. soppresade
¼ lb. Genoa salami
2 pkg. basket cheese, sliced
1 lb. sliced mozzarella
2 pieces of pizza dough or bread dough (*pizza dough is easier to work with*)

Beat eggs. Mix ricotta, black pepper and large handful of grating cheese, then mix into egg mixture. Mix all together with mixer. If mixture is too thick, add a little milk.

Line bottom of square pan with layer of dough over lapping the edges of the pan. Put a layer of ricotta mixture and spread. Overlap a layer of cheese, a layer of sausage and a layer of soppresade.

Repeat another layer of ricotta mixture, a layer of cheese, prosciutto, pepperoni, and Genoa salami. Repeat another layer of ricotta mixture, cheese, hard sausage, soppresade, then a layer of pepperoni or salami. Repeat another layer of ricotta mixture, cheese, prosciutto, and then layer whatever is left.

Top with another layer of ricotta mixture. Put top piece of dough on and roll the edges. Make holes in the dough with a fork. Dot top and rub edges with margarine. Bake at 350 degrees for 1½ to 2 hours or until toothpick comes out clean.

Easter Bread

1 pkg. active dry yeast
1¼ c. warm water
2 tsp. sugar
2 tsp. oil
4½ c. flour
2 eggs
1 egg yolk, beaten with 1 tsp. water
colored hard boiled eggs

In a large mixing bowl, sprinkle yeast over ¼ cup of the warm water. Let stand until soft, about 5 minutes. Add remaining one cup of warm water, sugar and lo. Mix in 3 cups of the flour and beat at medium speed until smooth approximately 5 minutes (*can do by hand if you choose*). Beat in egg, one at a time, and gradually stir in 1½ cups of flour to make a soft dough.

Turn dough out onto a floured board and knead until dough is smooth and satiny and small bubbles form just under the surface. Add more flour if dough becomes sticky.

Turn dough into a greased bowl. Cover and let rise in a warm place until doubled, about 1 hour. Punch dough down, cover again and let rise until doubled, about 45 minutes. Punch down and divide into 3 equal portions.

On a lightly floured board, troll each portion into an 18-inch strand. Place the 3 strands on greased baking sheet and braid, pinching the ends together. Let rise until doubled, about 45 minutes. Brush with egg yolk mixture and add colored eggs. Bake at 375 degrees for about 45 minutes or until crust is golden brown and loaf sounds hollow when tapped.

Momma's
FAVORITE DRINKS

Chocolate Egg Cream

2 oz. chocolate syrup
4 oz. cold milk
6 oz. cold seltzer

Use a 12-ounce glass. Pour in chocolate syrup, then stir in milk. Tilt glass and squirt seltzer making a foam on top. Drink immediately.

Homemade Limoncello

1 liter 100 proof vodka
1 liter water
4 c. sugar
zest of 10 to 12 lemons

Wash lemons with a brush to clean thoroughly. Zest the lemons so there is no white on the peel. Place the zest in a bowl and add the vodka. Place in cool place and let sit for at least 4 days. The longer it sits the more of the flavor of the lemon flavor melds into the vodka.

In a large saucepan, combine water and sugar and cook until sugar dissolves and thickens about 10 minutes. Allow the liquid to cool before adding the limoncello mixture. Cover with plastic wrap and let mixture sit for at least 10 days. Then strain the zest and bottle the mixture. Store in freezer until ready to serve.

Homemade Rock & Rye

1 liter rye whiskey
6 oz. rock candy
orange slices

In a large clear bottle add whiskey, rock candy and orange slices.

Allow to set for at least 7 days in a cool dry place before serving. The longer the rock candy sits, the better the flavor.

Momma's Grandkids

Among the older Italian women, there is an unwritten custom that when your husband passes away, you wear black forever. Momma carried on that tradition until the day she died.

She lived five years after the death of her husband and wore black all those years. It is the ultimate respect a widow pays to her husband.

Her life after Poppa was concentrated on her twelve grandchildren. She had a special relationship with each one and showered her love upon them. She showed that love through the art of her cooking. She would prepare food for them in imaginative ways. For breakfast, she would take a slice of bread, cut a hole in it with a glass and fry an egg in the center. Her French toast consisted of a cream cheese and jelly sandwich dipped in egg batter and then fried. The kids loved it. She would serve it to them with her subtle smile and a wink, thus communicating it was made special for them. Today her grandchildren prepare breakfast for their own children in the very same manner.

Missing Momma

When Momma passed away, we lost a generation that knew the meaning of family tradition. Although we carry on many of her traditions, the family chain has been broken. Children have a way of going their own way, especially when they have their own children and grandchildren. Though our families have grown, values Momma taught us will hopefully perpetuate to the next generation.

The best gift we can give our families are our treasured customs and traditions. Momma gave us love. This love was expressed by everything she did. Whether it was the way she cooked, kept her home, or cared for her husband and children; her labor was a labor of love. This is her legacy. It is our turn to treasure and preserve them and give our children the same sense of family values for future generations.

To all those years we shared and all the ones we continue to share, we will always remember that very special lady.

Momma, we miss you very much.

Weights & Measures

Liquid Volume

Dash or pinch	less than ⅛ teaspoon
3 teaspoons	1 tablespoon
4 tablespoons	¼ cup
8 tablespoons	½ cup
16 tablespoons	1 cup
2 cups	1 pint
4 cups	1 quart
4 quarts	1 gallon
16 ounces	1 pound
32 ounces	1 quart

Dry Weight

16 ounces = 1 pound
1 ounce = 28.35 grams
1 pound = 454 grams
1 gram = 0.035 ounce
1 kilogram = 2.2 pounds

Equivalents

Butter: 2 tablespoons = 1 ounce
8 tablespoons = ¼ pound
1 cup = ½ pound
Flour: 4 cups = 1 pound
Herbs: 1 tablespoon = 1teaspoon dried
Sugar: 2 cups = 1 pound

About the Author

Arlene Iaquinto was born in the Bronx, New York, to a middle class Italian family. She developed her love for cooking from her mother-in-law, Lucia Franco. While observing Lucia's passion for preparing special dishes for her family during the Christmas holiday, Arlene developed the same passion for meal preparation not only during the holidays but whenever family would gather for meals. This strong sense of family and love of cooking prompted her to write down the recipes handed down to her by Lucia. Arlene shares the traditions of an Italian family hopes to pass those traditions and her love of cooking that Lucia inspired to others through this book.

To contact the author or order additional gift copies of this book, visit: *www.MommasChristmas.com.*